Holiness

The Fullness in Christ

Insights From the Epistle to the Colossians

SPIRITUAL JOURNEY SERIES

Holiness

The Fullness in Christ

Insights From the Epistle to the Colossians

✝ ShineInternational

SPIRITUAL JOURNEY SERIES:
Holiness & The Fullness in Christ

Copyright © 2024 Shine International
First edition August 2024
Published by Shine International
Phoenix, Arizona
Email: shinebooksmedia@gmail.com
Website: www.shineinternational.org

ISBN 978-1-962580-03-8

For in Him dwells all the fullness of the Godhead bodily;
and you are complete in Him,
who is the head of all principality and power.

Colossians 2:9, 10

CONTENTS

About This Series

T his series consists of a collection of short spiritual talks about various fundamental topics that lay an important foundation for the believers in their spiritual life, growth, and journey. The short books in this series explore these fundamental topics from a biblical and spiritual understanding, that the believer may build on a solid foundation (Matthew 7:24).

These messages were originally delivered over the years to a spiritual community dedicated to living the Christian life in a genuine and scriptural way, growing in the life in Christ and in the Spirit.

This book is the first book in this series, exploring two of the most foundational topics: *holiness and the fullness in Christ.*

Holiness

Introduction

H oliness is essential in the life of God's people. It is not, as some may think, a quality related only to spiritually advanced people, but it is an essential quality that ought to be acquired by all believers, as the writer to the Hebrews says: *'Pursue peace with all people, and <u>holiness, without which no one will see the Lord</u>'* (Hebrews 12:14).

The phrase, *'Be holy, for I am holy'*, which signifies a commandment, is mentioned eight times in the Bible.[1]

This book consists of three main parts that will take you on a brief journey through the books of Scripture to help you understand God's mind regarding holiness:

Part 1: Basic Principles

Part 2: Holiness is a Journey

Part 3: Holiness is a Process of Sanctification

---

[1] Leviticus 11:44, 45; 19:2; 20:7, 26; 21:8; 1 Peter 1:15, 16

Part 1

Basic Principles

I. The Meaning of Holiness

1. Being cut off from worldly and profane matters

In 2 Corinthians 6:14–7:1, we read:

> Do not be unequally yoked together with unbelievers. For
> what fellowship has righteousness with lawlessness? And
> what communion has light with darkness? And what accord
> has Christ with Belial? Or what part has a believer with an
> unbeliever? And what agreement has the temple of God with
> idols? For you are the temple of the living God. As God has
> said: "I will dwell in them and walk among them. I will be
> their God, and they shall be My people." Therefore "Come
> out from among them and be separate, says the Lord. Do not
> touch what is unclean, and I will receive you." "I will be a
> Father to you, and you shall be My sons and daughters, says
> the Lord Almighty." Therefore, having these promises, be-
> loved, let us cleanse ourselves from all filthiness of the flesh
> and spirit, perfecting holiness in the fear of God.

Unfortunately, many unclean things enter the life of God's
people and God's Holy Church. In Micah 1:7–9, we read:

> All her carved images shall be beaten to pieces, and all her
> pay as a harlot shall be burned with the fire; all her idols I
> will lay desolate, for she gathered it from the pay of a harlot,

and they shall return to the pay of a harlot. Therefore I will wail and howl, I will go stripped and naked; I will make a wailing like the jackals and a mourning like the ostriches, for her wounds are incurable. <u>For it has come to Judah; it has come to the gate of My people—to Jerusalem.</u>

2. Set apart

The Lord called the nation of Israel to be holy and set apart for Him:

Now therefore, if you will indeed obey My voice and keep My covenant, then <u>you shall be a special treasure to Me above all people;</u> for all the earth is Mine. <u>And you shall be to Me a kingdom of priests and a holy nation</u> (Exodus 19:5, 6).

However, 40 days after God made a covenant with them, they unfortunately went astray and worshipped the calf:

And Moses said to Aaron, "What did this people do to you that you have brought so great a sin upon them?" So Aaron said, "Do not let the anger of my lord become hot. You know the people, that they are set on evil. For they said to me, 'Make us gods that shall go before us; as for this Moses, the man who brought us out of the land of Egypt, we do not know what has become of him.' And I said to them, 'Whoever has any gold, let them break it off.' So they gave it to me, and I cast it into the fire, and this calf came out." Now when Moses saw that the people were unrestrained (for Aaron had not *restrained them, to their shame among their enemies), then Moses stood in the entrance of the camp, and said, "<u>Whoever is on the Lord's side—come to me</u>!" And all the sons of Levi gathered themselves together to him. And he said to them, "Thus says the Lord God of Israel: 'Let every man put his sword on his side, and go in and out from entrance to entrance throughout the camp, and let every man kill his brother, every man his companion, and every man his neighbour.' " So the sons of Levi did according to the word of Moses. And about three thousand men of the people fell that day. Then Moses said, "<u>Consecrate yourselves today to the Lord</u>, that He may bestow on you a blessing this day, for every man has opposed his son and his brother"* (Exodus 32:21–29).

Notice the cry of Moses: *'Whoever is on the Lord's side—come to me!'* At that time, the tribe of Levi was chosen to be set apart for the Lord.

Holiness is a serious calling. It protects the people from being smitten by a curse or a plague. In Numbers 8:19, we read:

And I have given the Levites as a gift to Aaron and his sons from among the children of Israel, to do the work for the children of Israel in the tabernacle of meeting, and to make atonement for the children of Israel, <u>that there be no plague among the children of Israel</u> when the children of Israel come near the sanctuary.

But it is also costly, as we have just read in Exodus 32:27.

Also, in Deuteronomy 33:8–11, we read:

> And of Levi he said: "Let Your Thummim and Your Urim be with Your holy one, whom You tested at Massah, and with whom You contended at the waters of Meribah, <u>who says of his father and mother, 'I have not seen them'; nor did he acknowledge his brothers, or know his own children; for they have observed Your word and kept Your covenant</u>. They shall teach Jacob Your judgments, and Israel Your law. They shall put incense before You, and a whole burnt sacrifice on Your altar. Bless his substance, Lord, and accept the work of his hands; strike the loins of those who rise against him, and of those who hate him, that they rise not again."

Then, in the New Testament, God restored His original plan, where the whole Church is a spiritual tribe of Levi. In 1 Peter 2:9, we read:

> But you are a chosen generation, a royal priesthood, <u>a holy nation</u>, His own special people, that you may proclaim the praises of Him who called you out of darkness into His marvellous light.

Again, there is a cost for this separation and setting apart.

In Luke 14:26, we read:

If anyone comes to Me and does not hate his father and mother, wife and children, brothers and sisters, yes, and his own life also, he cannot be My disciple.

Also, in 2 Corinthians 5:16, we read:

Therefore, from now on, we regard no one according to the flesh. Even though we have known Christ according to the flesh, yet now we know Him thus no longer.

Then, in 2 Corinthians 6:16–17, we read:

And what agreement has the temple of God with idols? For you are the temple of the living God. As God has said: "I will dwell in them and walk among them. I will be their God, and they shall be My people." Therefore "Come out from among them and be separate, says the Lord. Do not touch what is unclean, and I will receive you."

It is a challenging responsibility. If we bear this responsibility and follow its standards, we can stand in the gap on behalf of the world and the Church of God.

3. Wholesomeness and health

Just as our bodies need certain elements such as nutrition, air, lack of pollution, and medical care to be healthy, our spirits need holiness as an atmosphere to remain healthy.

II. God Requires His People to be Holy Because He is Holy

In 2 Corinthians 7:1, we read:

Therefore, having these promises, beloved, let us cleanse ourselves from all filthiness of the flesh and spirit, perfecting holiness in the fear of God.

Because of His desire to make us holy, God took the initiative and provided all we needed to acquire holiness. He gave us:

- The blood of Jesus—redemption
- The Holy Spirit who sanctifies us continuously

In 1 Thessalonians 4:3, 7–8, we read:

For this is the will of God, your sanctification: that you should abstain from sexual immorality ... For God did not call us to uncleanness, but in holiness. Therefore he who rejects this does not reject man, but God, who has also given us His Holy Spirit.

Also, in 1 Peter 1:2, we read:

Elect according to the foreknowledge of God the Father, in sanctification of the Spirit, for obedience <u>and sprinkling of the blood of Jesus Christ</u>: Grace to you and peace be multiplied.

Therefore, the Bible calls the believers *saints*, meaning *holy people*:

> *To the church of God which is at Corinth, to those who are sanctified in Christ Jesus, <u>called to be saints</u>, with all who in every place call on the name of Jesus Christ our Lord, both theirs and ours* (1 Corinthians 1:2).

> *Just as He chose us in Him before the foundation of the world, <u>that we should be holy</u> and without blame before Him in love* (Ephesians 1:4).

> *Therefore, as <u>the elect of God, holy and beloved</u>, put on tender mercies, kindness, humility, meekness, longsuffering* (Colossians 3:12).

> *But as He who called you is holy, <u>you also be holy</u> in all your conduct, because it is written, "Be holy, for I am holy"* (1 Peter 1:15,16).

> *But you are a chosen generation, a royal priesthood, <u>a holy nation</u>, His own special people, that you may proclaim the praises of Him who called you out of darkness into His marvellous light* (1 Peter 2:9).

> *Who has saved us and <u>called us with a holy calling</u>, not according to our works, but according to His own purpose and grace which was given to us in Christ Jesus before time began* (2 Timothy 1:9).

III. The Purpose of Being Holy and God's Mind Concerning This Calling to Holiness

The purpose of this calling to holiness is manifold. We will only mention a few points here:

1. God desires to dwell among His people

God is Omnipresent, meaning that He is present everywhere. Yet He desires to dwell literally among His people whom He loves and has called to be His own. However, for this to happen, His people ought to prepare a dwelling place for Him and they ought to be holy in order for Him to dwell in their midst. This matter is highlighted repeatedly in Scripture, as clear in the following references:

> *And let them make Me a sanctuary, <u>that I may dwell among them</u>* (Exodus 25:8).

> *This shall be a continual burnt offering throughout your generations at the door of the tabernacle of meeting before the Lord, where I will meet you to speak with you. And there I will meet with the children of Israel, and the tabernacle shall be sanctified by My glory. So I will consecrate the tabernacle of meeting and the altar. I will also consecrate both Aaron and his sons to minister to Me as priests. <u>I will dwell among the children of Israel and will be their God</u>. And they shall*

know that I am the Lord their God, who brought them up out of the land of Egypt, <u>that I may dwell among them</u>. I am the Lord their God (Exodus 29:42–46).

And the Lord spoke to Moses, saying: "Command the children of Israel that they put out of the camp every leper, everyone who has a discharge, and whoever becomes defiled by a corpse. You shall put out both male and female; you shall put them outside the camp, <u>that they may not defile their camps in the midst of which I dwell</u>" (Numbers 5:1–3).

For the Lord <u>your God walks in the midst of your camp</u>, to deliver you and give your enemies over to you; <u>therefore your camp shall be holy</u>, that He may see no unclean thing among you, and turn away from you (Deuteronomy 23:14).

Moreover I will make a covenant of peace with them, and it shall be an everlasting covenant with them; I will establish them and multiply them, and <u>I will set My sanctuary in their midst forevermore</u>. My tabernacle also shall be with them; indeed I will be their God, and they shall be My people. The nations also will know that I, the Lord, sanctify Israel, when My sanctuary is in their midst forevermore (Ezekiel 37: 26–28).

Sing and rejoice, O daughter of Zion! For behold, <u>I am coming and I will dwell in your midst</u>," says the Lord. "Many nations shall be joined to the Lord in that day, and they shall become My people. And <u>I will dwell in your midst</u>. Then you will know that the Lord of hosts has sent Me to you. And the

Lord will take possession of Judah as His inheritance in the Holy Land, and will again choose Jerusalem" (Zechariah 2:10–12).

The example of the Tabernacle helps us understand this point about God's general presence and His literal or actual presence amid His people. Outside the Tabernacle was God's general presence; however, inside the Tabernacle, there was a special and awesome presence of God as highlighted in the following references:

Then the cloud covered the tabernacle of meeting, and the glory of the Lord filled the tabernacle. And Moses was not able to enter the tabernacle of meeting, because the cloud rested above it, and the glory of the Lord filled the tabernacle (Exodus 40:34–35).

And it came to pass, when the priests came out of the holy place, that the cloud filled the house of the Lord, so that the priests could not continue ministering because of the cloud; for the glory of the Lord filled the house of the Lord (1 Kings 8:10–11).

But why does God want to dwell amid His people?

– He loves us and wants to share His life with us:

Rejoicing in His inhabited world, and my delight was with the sons of men (Proverbs 8:31).

By which have been given to us exceedingly great and pre-cious promises, that through these <u>you may be partakers of the divine nature</u>, having escaped the corruption that is in the world through lust (2 Peter 1:4).

— He seeks a headquarters from where He can run His Kingdom affairs

God can accomplish all His work alone, but He loves to work with us and wants us to partake in His work:

We then, <u>as workers together with Him also</u> plead with you not to receive the grace of God in vain (2 Corinthians 6:1).

— A warning

We ought to take the divine presence seriously and be aware that God is fire; therefore, this fire can quickly con-sume any unholy things or persons. Remember the story of Ananias and Sapphira in Acts 5:1–11.

There were also similar experiences in the early centuries. This happened often in the deserts of Egypt, where the wor-shippers were aware that they ought to prepare a dwelling place for God. Therefore, God literally dwelt among them to the extent that any demon-possessed person sent into the desert to be delivered would usually hardly reach the worshippers' abode, but from a distance of still a few miles away, the evil spirits would sense the literal presence of God from afar off and cry out, "Fire! Fire!" and they would de-part from the person.

Sometimes the dirt and filthiness of the world come into our lives; therefore, we may need the fire of the Lord to come and cleanse us. But in this case, it would be the fire of judgement, not the fire of His indwelling. This point is highlighted in Scripture as follows:

> *Therefore thus says the Lord God: "Woe to the bloody city, to the pot whose scum is in it, and whose scum is not gone from it! Bring it out piece by piece, on which no lot has fallen. For her blood is in her midst; she set it on top of a rock; she did not pour it on the ground, to cover it with dust. That it may raise up fury and take vengeance, I have set her blood on top of a rock, that it may not be covered." 'Therefore thus says the Lord God: "Woe to the bloody city! I too will make the pyre great. Heap on the wood, kindle the fire; cook the meat well, mix in the spices, and let the cuts be burned up. "Then set the pot empty on the coals, that it may become hot and its bronze may burn, that its filthiness may be melted in it, that its scum may be consumed. She has grown weary with lies, and her great scum has not gone from her. Let her scum be in the fire! In your filthiness is lewdness. Because I have cleansed you, and you were not cleansed, you will not be cleansed of your filthiness anymore, till I have caused My fury to rest upon you. I, the Lord, have spoken it; it shall come to pass, and I will do it; I will not hold back, nor will I spare, nor will I relent; according to your ways and according to your deeds they will judge you," says the Lord God'* (Ezekiel 24:6–14).

Therefore, since we are receiving a kingdom which cannot be shaken, let us have grace, by which we may serve God acceptably with reverence and godly fear. <u>For our God is a consuming fire</u> (Hebrews 12:28, 29).

"So it was, when you heard the voice from the midst of the darkness, while the mountain was burning with fire, that you came near to me, all the heads of your tribes and your elders. And you said: 'Surely the Lord our God has shown us His glory and His greatness, and we have heard His voice from the midst of the fire. We have seen this day that God speaks with man; yet he still lives. Now therefore, why should we die? <u>For this great fire will consume us</u>; if we hear the voice of the Lord our God anymore, then we shall die. For who is there of all flesh who has heard the voice of the living God speaking from the midst of the fire, as we have, and lived? You go near and hear all that the Lord our God may say, and tell us all that the Lord our God says to you, and we will hear and do it.' "Then the Lord heard the voice of your words when you spoke to me, and the Lord said to me: 'I have heard the voice of the words of this people which they have spoken to you. They are right in all that they have spoken. Oh, that they had such a heart in them that they would fear Me and always keep all My commandments, that it might be well with them and with their children forever!'" (Deuteronomy 5:23–29).

2. To reflect God's character to the other nations so that these nations might be drawn to God

We must remember that the message of the gospel is not only to be heard but ought also to be seen. Therefore, we ought to be a living or an incarnate gospel so that the Holy Spirit may work powerfully with us.

In Acts 5:32, we read:

> And _we are His witnesses_ to these things, and so also is the Holy Spirit whom God has given to those who obey Him.

We are called to be examples for others—to be christs!

In Matthew 5:48, we read:

> Therefore you shall be perfect, _just as_ your Father in heaven is perfect.

Also, in Romans 8:29, we read:

> For whom He foreknew, He also predestined _to be conformed to the image of His Son_, that He might be the firstborn among many brethren.

In Hebrews 12:10, we read:

> For they indeed for a few days chastened us as seemed best to them, but He for our profit, _that we may be partakers of His holiness_.

In 1 John 3:2–3, we read:

> *Beloved, now we are children of God; and it has not yet been revealed what we shall be, but we know that when He is revealed, we shall be like Him, for we shall see Him as He is. And everyone who has this hope in Him <u>purifies himself, just as He is pure</u>.*

3. Holy people sanctify the world through restricting and opposing the stream of transgression

In 2 Thessalonians 2:7, we read:

> *For the mystery of lawlessness is already at work; only He who now restrains will do so until He is taken out of the way.*

There is a strong stream of transgression caused by the enemy in his attempt to pollute every area in society and even pollute the Church of God so that he can subdue the earth to his dominion.

The holy people of God ought to stand as an opposing power that restrains this evil stream. It is the responsibility of pastors to guard their flock and the responsibility of parents to guard their children. They ought to stand as doorkeepers, preventing this evil activity from passing on to their flock.

Jesus said in John 14:30, *'I will no longer talk much with you, for the ruler of this world is coming, and he has nothing in Me.'*

St. Gregory, the theologian (4th century), was ordained bishop over a parish that only had seven believers; however, at the end of his life when he reposed in the Lord, he left his parish with only seven non-believers. He learned the secret of standing against the stream of transgression and blocking every evil activity and plan from the enemy.

4. Holiness is a requirement of acceptable worship

In Matthew 15:7–9, we read:

> *"Hypocrites! Well did Isaiah prophesy about you, saying: 'These people draw near to Me with their mouth, and honour Me with their lips, but their heart is far from Me. And in vain they worship Me, teaching as doctrines the commandments of men.'"*

Also, in Romans 12:1, we read:

> *I beseech you therefore, brethren, by the mercies of God, that you present your bodies a living sacrifice, holy, acceptable to God, which is your reasonable service.*

In Hebrews 10:19–22, we read:

> *Therefore, brethren, having boldness to enter the Holiest by the blood of Jesus, by a new and living way which He consecrated for us, through the veil, that is, His flesh, and having*

a High Priest over the house of God, let us draw near with a true heart in full assurance of faith, having our hearts sprinkled from an evil conscience and our bodies washed with pure water.

Holiness grants spiritual energy that carries one's prayers to the throne of God without any hindrance. We all know the story in Daniel 10:

But <u>the prince of the kingdom of Persia withstood me twenty-one days</u>; and behold, <u>Michael, one of the chief princes, came to help me</u>, for I had been left alone there with the kings of Persia (Daniel 10:13).

IV. Practically, Holiness Can Be Discussed on Two Levels

1. Personal

2. Corporate

1. On the personal level

Holiness is a process; it is a walk with God that is based on God's redemptive gift—His grace. We receive this gift from the very beginning of our walk with Christ.

In Ephesians 1:3, we read:

> Blessed be the God and Father of our Lord Jesus Christ, who has _blessed us with every spiritual blessing_ in the heavenly places in Christ.

However, this gift is deposited in our spirits like a jewel in a closed box. Our responsibility is to work out this gift of holiness, by opening the box and allowing the jewel inside it to shine through our entire being—our spirit, soul, and body.[2]

---

[2] This point will be further explained in the course of the book.

2. On the corporate level

The corporate level focuses on how the Church of God lives and reflects God's holiness. Some important highlights in this respect:

- Integrity of the lives of her members
- Fellowship of love and light
- Transparency in finances

Two important biblical passages ought to be highlighted in this context:

- Ephesians 5:1–21
- 1 John 1:5–9

- ## Ephesians 5:1–21

Therefore be imitators of God as dear children. And walk in love, as Christ also has loved us and given Himself for us, an offering and a sacrifice to God for a sweet-smelling aroma. But fornication and all uncleanness or covetousness, let it not even be named among you, as is fitting for saints; neither filthiness, nor foolish talking, nor coarse jesting, which are not fitting, but rather giving of thanks. For this you know, that no fornicator, unclean person, nor covetous man, who is an idolater, has any inheritance in the kingdom of Christ and God. Let no one deceive you with empty words, for because of these things the wrath of God comes upon the sons of disobedience. Therefore do not be partakers with them. For you were once darkness, but now you are light in the Lord. Walk as children of light (for the fruit of the Spirit is in all goodness, righteousness, and truth), finding out what is acceptable to the Lord. And have no fellowship with the unfruitful works of darkness, but rather expose them. For it is shameful even to speak of those things which are done by them in secret. But all things that are exposed are made manifest by the light, for whatever makes manifest is light. Therefore He says: "Awake, you who sleep, arise from the dead, and Christ will give you light." See then that you walk circumspectly, not as fools but as wise, redeeming the time, because the days are evil. Therefore do not be unwise, but understand what the will of the Lord is. And do not be drunk with wine, in which is dissipation; but be filled with the Spirit, speaking to one another in psalms and hymns and spiritual songs, singing and making melody in your heart to the Lord, giving thanks always for all things to God the Father in the name of our Lord Jesus Christ, submitting to one another in the fear of God.

The key word in this passage is *walk*:

- Walk in love (verse 2): How? Sacrifice (verses 1–2).
- Walk in light (verse 8): How? Purity—avoid unclean things (verses 3–14).
- Walk in wisdom (verse 15): How? Redeem the time.

- **1 John 1:5–9**

  This is the message which we have heard from Him and declare to you, that God is light and in Him is no darkness at all. If we say that we have fellowship with Him, and walk in darkness, we lie and do not practise the truth. But if we walk in the light as He is in the light, we have fellowship with one another, and the blood of Jesus Christ His Son cleanses us from all sin. If we say that we have no sin, we deceive ourselves, and the truth is not in us. If we confess our sins, He is faithful and just to forgive us our sins and to cleanse us from all unrighteousness.

We need this fellowship with one another because it enables each of us to see areas we cannot otherwise see on our own—our blind spot.

Part 2

Holiness is a Journey

Holiness is a journey in the fear of the Lord, as we read in 2 Corinthians 7:1:

> *Therefore, having these promises, beloved, let us cleanse ourselves from all filthiness of the flesh and spirit, <u>perfecting holiness in the fear of God</u>.*

It is a walk or a journey in a holy lifestyle and holy conduct. It is *the art of a special walk with God*, in which He daily sanctifies us by the Holy Spirit as we walk with Him in obedience.

This journey reminds us of a toddler learning to walk, as physical and spiritual matters are always parallel. Just as our parents cared for us and taught us how to walk, our heavenly Father also teaches us. However, we must be obedient, not stubborn.

To examine our walk, we ought to ask ourselves a couple of questions. First, do we move forward or do we spin in circles in our walk? Also, do we continue walking in fellowship with the Lord during the day or do we hurriedly leave the Lord behind after finishing our morning quiet time, get immersed in our daily activities, and hence the flesh quickly surfaces?

When we decide to prioritise walking in holiness as the most important thing in our lives, the Holy Spirit draws near us, leads us, teaches us, and protects us from the defilement around us.

When we honour God, He entrusts us with the great matters of His Kingdom.

The main emphasis of the Bible is actually on holiness, not on the love of God. Theologically, it is said: "Love is central in God, but holiness is central in love!"

God's love is holy, not emotional as our love, because God is light (1 John 1:5) and God is love (1 John 4:8, 16).

The Hebrew word for *holy*, used in Leviticus, means *set apart*. The English word *holy* comes from the old English word *halig*, which means to be wholesome and healthy. The related word *sanctify* comes from the Latin *sanctus*, which means consecrated, sacred, or blameless. The word *sanctification* describes the process of becoming Christlike, and the word *holy* describes the result of this process.

- **God revealed Himself in holiness**

  o On Mount Sinai

  Now all the people witnessed the thunderings, the lightning flashes, the sound of the trumpet, and the mountain smoking; and when the people saw it, they trembled and stood afar off (Exodus 20:18).

o   God is glorious in holiness

"Who is like You, O LORD, among the gods? Who is like You, glorious in holiness, fearful in praises, doing wonders?" (Exodus 15:11).

o   *The Holy One of Israel* is one of the repeated names of Jehovah in the Scriptures

In Isaiah alone this phrase is used 30 times.

[In the Book of Leviticus, the word *holy* is used 91 times. We may think this is a book solely for the Levites and priests but, in fact, Apostle Peter quotes the key verse of this book, *'Be holy, for I am holy'* (1 Peter 1:15,16). There are also more than 100 quotes from Leviticus in the New Testament.]

- ## What do we encounter on our journey towards holiness?

We may think that when we make the decision to walk in holiness, we will soon experience the presence of the Lord accompanying us. But this is not necessarily the case because we may first encounter the enemy's opposition. The enemy hates, or rather, fears those who walk in holiness. As a result, the person encounters a great deal of difficulties at the beginning of the walk and the journey to holiness.

This experience is sometimes referred to as the great and terrible wilderness (Deuteronomy 1:19) or the dark night of the soul—a term used by St. John of the Cross (16th century).

God allows this opposition of the enemy, which is always under His control, and uses it to perform, as it were, a major surgery in our inner life. What matters for God is not what we can do in His Kingdom but what we can reflect of His Person so that He can come and dwell in us. In John 14:23, Jesus said: *"'If anyone loves Me, he will keep My word; and My Father will love him, and <u>We will come to him and make Our home with him.</u>'"*

In Ephesians 3:17, we read: *'<u>That Christ may dwell in your hearts</u> through faith; that you, being rooted and grounded in love.'*

Also, in Galatians 4:19, we read: *'My little children, for whom I labour in birth again <u>until Christ is formed in you</u>.'*

Three biblical examples of patriarchs, prophets, and apostles—Abraham, Isaiah, and Paul

- **Abraham (Genesis 15)**

Abraham obeyed God. He left everything and went to the place appointed by God. But He found nothing. Even God who had been so near and His voice so clear seemed far or absent at some point.

Then, problems began, including a famine, going to Egypt and all that happened there, the strife between Abraham's herdsmen and Lot's herdsmen, and a battle to rescue Lot after he was taken captive. The years were passing without seeing the promised offspring and the promised land.

Despite this, unlike what we often do, Abraham continued in his fellowship with the Lord, always keeping an altar, which is a sign of his fellowship with God, and always living in a tent, which is a symbol of keeping himself separate from all that might defile him—the gods of the surrounding nations and people's habits.

At that time, while his fears began to augment and sadness crept into his life, God appeared to him (Genesis 15). God addressed him directly, exposing his troubles and struggles: fear, having no descendants, and having no land to possess.

– Fear (verse 1)

After these things the word of the Lord came to Abram in a vision, saying, "Do not be afraid, Abram. I am your shield, your exceedingly great reward" (Genesis 15:1).

The Lord said to Abraham not to fear because God was his shield. If any battle or enemies would rise against him, God would be with him and would be his shield. Hence, no harm could touch him.

– Descendants (verses 2–6)

As it were, the Lord was saying to Abraham:

Come out, not only of your tent to look at the sky and the stars, but also out of the prison of your fears and thoughts.

Come out of the narrow world you made for yourself and the small God you imagined in your thoughts.

Come and see how great God is. He is the Creator of all this vast world and all these stars.

– The land (verses 7–17)

God instructed Abraham to prepare some animals in a certain way. Abraham would quickly understand what this meant because it was the custom of his time for entering into a covenant. But what followed was remarkable.

Abraham was ready for God's appearance. He had prepared everything. However, God did not appear quickly and the vultures began to attack him. Again this reflects a picture of what the enemy tries to do in his final, desperate attempts. Abraham battled all day, from sunrise to sunset, then he fell asleep as he was extremely exhausted by the long battle.

Then God appeared in the form of fiery torches—light and fire.

Surprisingly enough, God did not ask Abraham to pass between the two parts of the animals, as the custom was for both parties to pass through. God said to Abraham that He Himself (God) would be the only one responsible for this covenant and that He would give him (Abraham) the land as He promised, to him and to his descendants.

- **Prophet Isaiah (Isaiah 50)**

In Isaiah 50:4–10, we read:

> *The Lord God has given Me the tongue of the learned, that I should know how to speak a word in season to him who is weary. He awakens Me morning by morning, He awakens My ear to hear as the learned. The Lord God has opened My ear; and I was not rebellious, nor did I turn away. <u>I gave My back to those who struck Me, and My cheeks to those who plucked out the beard; I did not hide My face from shame and spitting.</u> "For the Lord God will help Me; therefore I will not be disgraced; therefore I have set My face like a flint, and I know that I will not be ashamed. He is near who justifies Me; who will contend with Me? Let us stand together. Who is My adversary? Let him come near Me. Surely the Lord God will help Me; who is he who will condemn Me? Indeed they will all grow old like a garment; the moth will eat them up. "Who among you fears the Lord? Who obeys the voice of His Servant? <u>Who walks in darkness</u> and has no light? Let him trust in the name of the Lord and rely upon his God."*

When we read a prophetic passage related to the Messiah (Christ), we may think it belongs to Jesus only. However, usually the prophet who receives a prophetic word like this experiences it partially, otherwise, he would not be able to perceive, understand, or be entrusted with the prophetic word.

Thus, in this passage, we can envisage what the prophet Isaiah must have experienced. In verse 10, he speaks clearly about *the darkness*. Then, as we read through the subsequent chapters of the Book of Isaiah and reach chapter 53, we read the prophet's description of the crucifixion that is wonderfully and clearly portrayed. How did the prophet manage to convey this wonderful and clear description?

In fact, the prophet had gone through the valley of death—the dark night of the soul—and was thus able to climb the hill of Golgotha and see the day of the crucifixion.

Most of the prophets went through such an experience. It seems to be part of the prophetic calling in general. The fellowship in Christ's sufferings (Philippians 3:10) worked in the men of God in both Testaments and is still working to our days.

The life of Jeremiah is another picture of this fellowship in Christ's sufferings, as clear in his lamentations.

- **Apostle Paul**

After encountering the Lord on the way to Damascus, Apostle Paul began to preach the gospel. But he soon began to face many difficulties.

- He faced a humiliating experience as he was obliged to be dropped down the wall in a basket to escape death:

Now after many days were past, the Jews plotted to kill him. But their plot became known to Saul. And they watched the gates day and night, to kill him. Then the disciples took him by night and <u>let him down through the wall in a large basket</u> (Acts 9:23–25).

- He was not welcomed into the fellowship of the apostles until Barnabas interfered:

And when Saul had come to Jerusalem, he tried to join the disciples; but they were all afraid of him, and did not believe that he was a disciple. But Barnabas took him and brought him to the apostles. And he declared to them how he had seen the Lord on the road, and that He had spoken to him, and how he had preached boldly at Damascus in the name of Jesus (Acts 9:26, 27).

- He was exposed to plots to kill him and was obliged to go to Tarsus. This was a humbling experience because he had to go back to his family where he was not welcomed at all as he was a heretic in their eyes.

For 13 years, he was being trained in the divine school (three years in the Arabian deserts and 10 years in his region) and being prepared by God for the missionary work.

God was again, as it were, doing a major divine and spiritual surgical operation in the life of His apostle till he was transformed and said, *'it is no longer I who live, but Christ lives in me'* (Galatians 2:20).

He went through a great deal of suffering. In Acts 9:16, we read how the Lord said: *'For I will show him how many things he must suffer for My name's sake.'*

Also, in 2 Corinthians 11:16–33, we read the list of sufferings he went through for the sake of Christ. All these sufferings were under God's control and He used them to enable the apostle to carry out his mission as a messiah or a christ for his generation.

In 2 Corinthians 12:7–10, we read:

> *And lest I should be exalted above measure by the abundance of the revelations, a thorn in the flesh was given to me, a messenger of Satan to buffet me, lest I be exalted above measure. Concerning this thing I pleaded with the Lord three times that it might depart from me. And He said to me, "My grace is sufficient for you, for My strength is made perfect in weakness." Therefore most gladly I will rather boast in my infirmities, that the power of Christ may rest upon me. Therefore I take pleasure in infirmities, in reproaches, in needs, in persecutions, in distresses, for Christ's sake. For when I am weak, then I am strong.*

Not only did his mission field continuously expand from trip to trip but also his sufferings increased.

In Philippians 1:29, we read:

> *For to you it has been granted on behalf of Christ, not only to believe in Him, but also to suffer for His sake.*

Also, in Philippians 3:10, we read:

> *That I may know Him and the power of His resurrection, and the fellowship of His sufferings, being conformed to His death.*

Part 3

Holiness is a Process

of Sanctification

Introduction

As mentioned earlier, holiness is a grace or a gift grant-ed to us by God (Ephesians 1:3).

We need to work out this gift that we received, which is part of working out our salvation:

> *Therefore, my beloved, as you have always obeyed, not as in my presence only, but now much more in my absence, <u>work out your own salvation with fear and trembling</u>; for it is God who works in you both to will and to do for His good pleasure* (Philippians 2:12,13).

Without this grace, which is part of the grace of salvation (Ephesians 2:8), no one can achieve any degree of holiness.

But on the other hand, if we do not fulfil our role, the grace we receive will remain imprisoned in our spirits and the old nature will control our conduct because the old nature is dominant in our souls and minds.

Sanctification is a Process

We will discuss this point under four main titles:

    I.   Three basic lessons

II.   Three important truths

III.   Christlikeness—be a model, an icon, an incarnate gospel, a messiah, a small Christ

IV.   Practical steps

I.   Three Basic Lessons

1. Learn the art of self-denial

–   The key word here is to learn to say *No*

–   The key verse is Colossians 3:5:

Therefore put to death your members which are on the earth: fornication, uncleanness, passion, evil desire, and covetousness, which is idolatry.

2. Learn the art of sacrifice

–   The key word here is *be radical*

–   The key verse is Matthew 5:29

If your right eye causes you to sin, pluck it out and cast it from you; for it is more profitable for you that one of your members perish, than for your whole body to be cast into hell.

3. Learn the art of mutual delight

– The key word here is *plug in*

– The key verses are:

Delight yourself also in the Lord, and He shall give you the desires of your heart (Psalm 37:4).

Rejoicing in His inhabited world, and my delight was with the sons of men (Proverbs 8:31).

Let us discuss these three lessons in some detail.

1. The art of self-denial

Apostle Paul mentions a list of things that we ought to put to death by neglecting them and fleeing from them. There are certain things that can only be dealt with by ignoring them. If we try to deal with them by facing them, we increase their power.

It is important to learn how to ignore, neglect, or flee from spiritually harmful things. Apostle Paul advises Timothy to flee from such things, saying, *'Flee also youthful lusts'* (2 Timothy 2:22).

If we see that a certain emotion will end in any of the things Paul mentioned in Colossians 3:5, we should not harbour it inside. No one on earth is immune; we all know the things that we should not think about and should rather decide to neglect them and say *No* to them while staying humble and alert.

It is important to note here that, of course, we do not destroy sin by neglect. God deals with sin when we obey His commandments and respond to His dealings with us.

2. The art of sacrifice

The Bible speaks about *sacrifice* both in its chastening aspect and its worship aspect. The worship aspect means that I give back to God the best of what He has given me. In this way, He makes it His and mine forever.

What is the greatest thing that God has given me? It is *my right to myself*. In order to truly follow Jesus, I must give up my right to myself to Him, meaning to lay down my rights and put them on the altar.

By doing so, my natural passions are crucified with Christ and are transformed into sanctified passions.

In Matthew 5:29, Jesus seems to be very hard on us. He always healed the blind, and here He asks us to pluck out our eyes. However, it is not the physical eye that needs to be plucked out but the passion that controls the sight and opens the way to unclean and defiled things to enter and get hold of me, leaving me a captive to sin. Therefore, I need to be radical—to cut and sacrifice. I do this for God's sake, but, at the same time, this keeps me safe and holy. It is not only the wrong things that ought to be sacrificed but also the seemingly right things that stand in the way of my fellowship with the holy God.

Therefore, learn to be radical and call upon His grace to enable you. In Hebrews 4:16, it is written:

> *Let us therefore come boldly to the throne of grace, that we may obtain mercy and find grace to help in time of need.*

If this is difficult and seems to me that I cannot do it, this means I need to examine and review my love for Christ and if I truly love Him.

3. The art of mutual delight

The verses we read earlier highlight that Jesus is delighted in me and I am called to delight in Him.

It is like an electric circuit. When it is connected, the power flows and light comes in. Therefore, we need to learn to plug in!

When I am driven by fleshly desires, let me apply the art of mutual delight, let me plug in! Let me leave everything aside—my thoughts, enthusiasms, feelings, etcetera—and let my delight be in Him. Consequently, every wrong motivation will be exposed and corrected.

Let us learn to be like children. Jesus said, *'Unless you are converted and become as little children'* (Matthew 18:3). This means we ought to be simple hearted, have a simple eye, and lean on Him humbly and tenaciously.

II. Three Important Truths

1. Spiritual breathing (Isaiah 11:2, 3)

2. Heavenly citizenship (Philippians 3:20)

3. The grain of wheat (John 12:24)

1. Spiritual breathing

Breathing is the essence of life, both the physical and the spiritual. Our physical bodies need air in order to breathe and live. The air of the spirit is *the fear of God*. It is the medium that helps the spirit to live and grow. Without it, the spirit withers and becomes weak.

In Isaiah 11:2, 3, we read:

> *The Spirit of the Lord shall rest upon Him, the Spirit of wisdom and understanding, the Spirit of counsel and might, the Spirit of knowledge and of the fear of the Lord. <u>His delight is in the fear of the Lord</u>, and He shall not judge by the sight of His eyes, nor decide by the hearing of His ears.*

According to the original Hebrew language, the phrase 'His delight is in the fear of the Lord' literally reads 'He shall draw his breath in the fear of the Lord'.

Thus, the time we spend with the Lord connects us with His divine resources and allows His eternal life to flow into us, bringing His divine character inside us. In 2 Peter 1:4, we read:

> By which have been given to us exceedingly great and precious promises, that through these _you may be partakers of the divine nature_, having escaped the corruption that is in the world through lust.

2. A heavenly calling

The passport we carry reveals our citizenship and which country we belong to.

The Bible tells us that we have a heavenly citizenship:

> For _our citizenship is in heaven_, from which we also eagerly wait for the Saviour, the Lord Jesus Christ (Philippians 3:20).

This means that I ought to be a heavenly person. It is a call from God to live, walk, and behave as a heavenly person, having the traits or genes of my heavenly Father. In Matthew 5:48, it is written: 'Therefore you shall be perfect, just as your Father in heaven is perfect.'

This means that we ought to be sojourners on earth, waiting to finish our role and return home.

In 2 Corinthians 5:1–10, we read:

> For we know that if our earthly house, this tent, is destroyed, we have a building from God, a house not made with hands, eternal in the heavens. For in this we groan, earnestly desiring to be clothed with our habitation which is from heaven, if indeed, having been clothed, we shall not be found naked. For we who are in this tent groan, being burdened, not because we want to be unclothed, but further clothed, that mortality may be swallowed up by life. Now He who has prepared us for this very thing is God, who also has given us the Spirit as a guarantee. So we are always confident, knowing that while we are at home in the body we are absent from the Lord. For we walk by faith, not by sight. We are confident, yes, well pleased rather to be absent from the body and to be present with the Lord. Therefore we make it our aim, whether present or absent, to be well pleasing to Him. For we must all appear before the judgement seat of Christ, that each one may receive the things done in the body, according to what he has done, whether good or bad.

Jesus has ascended into heaven, taking us with Him and seating us in the heavenly places; therefore, the heavenly places have become our home. Yet, He sent us to earth for a mission. In John 20:21, we read: 'So Jesus said to them again, "Peace to you! As the Father has sent Me, _I also send you_."'

We need to focus on our mission to complete it as sojourners and return home.

3. The grain of wheat

The grain of wheat must die to bring forth more fruit.

Our dreams, visions, and the like may be put to death so that we may know our limitations and learn to lean on the Lord and continually receive life from its real source day after day. By this, we will not be living by our natural life (bios) but by the eternal life (zoe) granted to us:

> *Most assuredly, I say to you, he who hears My word and believes in Him who sent Me has everlasting life, and shall not come into judgement, but has passed from death into life. For as the Father has life in Himself, so He has granted the Son to have life in Himself* (John 5:24, 26).

> *The thief does not come except to steal, and to kill, and to destroy. I have come that they may have life, and that they may have it more abundantly* (John 10:10).

> *As You have given Him authority over all flesh, that He should give eternal life to as many as You have given Him. And this is eternal life, that they may know You, the only true God, and Jesus Christ whom You have sent* (John 17:2, 3).

This connects us with the vine and allows His sap to flow into us, bringing forth much fruit.

In John 15:4–6, we read:

> *Abide in Me, and I in you. As the branch cannot bear fruit of itself, unless it abides in the vine, neither can you, unless you abide in Me. "I am the vine, you are the branches. He who abides in Me, and I in him, bears much fruit; for without Me you can do nothing. If anyone does not abide in Me, he is cast out as a branch and is withered; and they gather them and throw them into the fire, and they are burned."*

III. Christlikeness

The aim of the process of sanctification is to be transformed into Christlikeness. In Romans 8:29, we read:

> *For whom He foreknew, He also predestined <u>to be conformed to the image of His Son</u>, that He might be the firstborn among many brethren.*

This means that we ought to be small christs or icons of Jesus, reflecting His Person and His life, not only His words!

Jesus is the icon of His Father (Hebrews 1:3), reflecting the Father's image because He is in full unity with the Father. When Jesus is formed in us, we too become His image or His icon, reflecting the life of Jesus to our world. Thus, the people will see a different picture, a different model, and a way of life different from theirs—one which challenges them to imitate it.

In Titus 2:14, we read:

Who gave Himself for us, that He might redeem us from every lawless deed and purify for Himself His own special people, zealous for good works.

Jesus always lived out what He taught.

In John 13:13–18, we read:

"You call Me Teacher and Lord, and you say well, for so I am. If I then, your Lord and Teacher, have washed your feet, you also ought to wash one another's feet. For I have given you an example, that you should do as I have done to you. Most assuredly, I say to you, a servant is not greater than his master; nor is he who is sent greater than he who sent him. If you know these things, blessed are you if you do them. "I do not speak concerning all of you. I know whom I have chosen; but that the Scripture may be fulfilled, 'He who eats bread with Me has lifted up his heel against Me."

Thus, Jesus was able to say:

Take My yoke upon you and learn from Me, for I am gentle and lowly in heart, and you will find rest for your souls (Matthew 11:29).

IV.   Practical Steps

Our aim is to:

1. Weaken the old nature

This can be done through:

- Fasting

- Daily repentance

- Submitting to God's chastening

- A sacrificial lifestyle and laying down our rights

2. Strengthen the new nature

This can be done through:

- Proper spiritual food and nourishment—milk or meat

But solid food belongs to those who are of full age, that is, those who by reason of use have their senses exercised to discern both good and evil (Hebrews 5:14).

- Psalms and prostrations

- The Word of God—learning to eat it

—　Stillness:

For thus says the Lord God, the Holy One of Israel: "In returning and rest you shall be saved; <u>in quietness</u> and confidence shall be your strength" (Isaiah 30:15).

<u>*Be still,*</u> *and know that I am God; I will be exalted among the nations, I will be exalted in the earth!* (Psalm 46:10).

<u>*Be silent,*</u> *all flesh, before the Lord, for He is aroused from His holy habitation!* (Zechariah 2:13).

—　Proclaiming the twelve statements of the Blood of Jesus and the Prophesying statements[3]

---

[3] Fr. Macarius (2017). *Prayers & Prophesying.* Shine International Inc. For the complete text of the Blood of Jesus statements and the Prophesying statements, refer to this book.

The Fullness in Christ

Insights From the Epistle to the Colossians

Readings

- ## Colossians 1:9–11

  For this reason we also, since the day we heard it, do not cease to pray for you, and to ask that you may be filled with the <u>knowledge of His will</u> in all wisdom and spiritual understanding; that you may walk worthy of the Lord, fully pleasing Him, being fruitful in every good work and increasing in the knowledge of God; strengthened with all might, according to His glorious power, for all patience and longsuffering with joy.

- ## Colossians 2:9, 10

  For in Him dwells all <u>the fullness of the Godhead</u> bodily; and you are complete in Him, who is the head of all principality and power.

- ## Colossians 3:17, 23

  And whatever you do in word or deed, do all in the name of the Lord Jesus, giving thanks to God the Father through Him … And whatever you do, do it heartily, as to the Lord and not to men.

- **Colossians 4:12**

    Epaphras, who is one of you, a bondservant of Christ, greets you, always labouring fervently for you in prayers, that you may stand perfect and complete in <u>all the will of God</u>.

Introduction

These passages highlight three essential truths, which are the subject of this message:

I.   The fullness of the Godhead (Colossians 2:9, 10)

II. The fullness of fruitfulness (Colossians 1:9, 11; 3:12–15; 3:17, 23)

III. The fullness of God's will (Colossians 1:9; 4:12)

I. The Fullness of the Godhead

E very believer in Christ is implanted in the body of Christ by the Holy Spirit:

> *For by one Spirit <u>we were all baptised into one body</u>— whether Jews or Greeks, whether slaves or free—and have all been made to drink into one Spirit* (1 Corinthians 12:13).

Therefore, we are branches in the vine (John 15:5), and the sap flows from the vine to each branch. However, some branches may be weak or withering due to some hindrances in these branches that obstruct the flow of the sap or due to the presence of thorns that absorb some of the sap, preventing it from reaching the branches. On the other hand, some branches are strong and fruitful.

Just as the sap flows from the vine to the branches, the life of Christ Himself—the divine life of the Son of God— flows to us and in us.

What is the nature of this divine life that flows in us?

The Epistle to the Colossians provides the answer to this question:

> *For in Him dwells all the fullness of the Godhead bodily* [in bodily form]; *and you are complete in Him, who is the head of all principality and power* (Colossians 2:9, 10).

This means that all the fullness of the Godhead dwells in the human body, which Christ took in His incarnation.

Since we are planted in Christ, this divine life, in its fullness, flows to us and within us.

What a great mystery and what a great gift! We have been granted the gift of the flow of Christ's nature—the divine nature—within us. This has been granted to us through a certain plan and economy. It does not mean that we will be divine like Christ. We will certainly not share in the essence of divinity, otherwise, we will be burned by its fire. But it means that divinity has been granted to us as a power that can change us so that we may be transformed into Christ-likeness.

The gift of divinity flows to us without stopping because there is no limit to God's gift. It is written:

> For God does not give the Spirit by measure (John 3:34).

> For the gifts and the calling of God are irrevocable (Romans 11:29).

The most important thing is to give this gift of divine life a chance to find a place inside us. This inner space becomes available as we grow spiritually. However, we should always watch over removing and clearing the hindrances. These hindrances may be bondages that need to be released or blockages that obstruct the flow of the sap. These hindrances can usually be removed through repentance. Yet, in addition to repentance, we need to renew our spiritual desires as the Psalmist says:

I opened my mouth and panted, for I longed for Your commandments (Psalm 119:131).

In another translation (WYC), this verse reads: *'I opened my mouth, and <u>drew the Spirit</u>.'*

Also, in Matthew 5:6, we read:

Blessed are those who hunger and thirst for righteousness, for they shall be filled.

The continuous inner flow of the divine life changes our lives completely. Also, this gift of divinity enables us to find answers to all our questions. The ability to understand and perceive these matters comes from the holy light of this gift of divinity that casts out darkness.

This gift of divinity also enables us to fulfil <u>all</u> the good, acceptable, and perfect will of God[4] in its manifold pictures.

The words *all* or *every* are repeated 24 times in the Epistle to the Colossians. Therefore:

For all questions, there are answers.

For every weakness, there is an enabling power.

For all confusion, there is a solution.

All stumbling will change into a true shaking and awakening.

---

[4] Romans 12:2

All these things come from the enabling power granted to us through the gift of divinity, as we read in Colossians 1:11: *'strengthened with all might, according to His glorious power'*. He is the source of the enabling power.

This truth about the gift of divinity is written of in other epistles as well, including the Epistle to the Hebrews and the Epistle of Second Peter. The divine truth is often presented in different ways so that we may be able to perceive its depth and live it out in its fullness.

In Hebrews 3:14, we read:

> For we have become <u>partakers of Christ</u> if we hold the beginning of our confidence steadfast to the end.

In the original Greek text, the word *partaker* here means *a sharer*.[5] Therefore, the word in this verse signifies a shared thing between us and Christ regarding His nature. It is, in fact, the gift of divinity discussed above.

Also, in 2 Peter 1:4, we read:

> By which have been given to us exceedingly great and precious promises, that through these you may be <u>partakers of the divine nature</u>, having escaped the corruption that is in the world through lust.

---

[5] Danker, F. W. (2000). A Greek-English Lexicon of the New Testament and Other Early Christian Literature. Third Edition (BDAG).

A different Greek word is used in this verse, but it also means *a sharer*. This word is used here to describe our partaking of the divine nature. According to the verse, it is a gift that has been granted to us by God in Christ. Through this gift, we can achieve this state of being partakers of His nature.

What is our responsibility towards this divine revelation of being partakers in the divine nature?

We can find the answer to this question in the same epistle.

After speaking about the gift of divinity (Colossians 2:9, 10), the apostle says:

> *In Him you were also circumcised with the circumcision made without hands, by putting off the body of the sins of the flesh, by the circumcision of Christ* (Colossians 2:11).

These words indicate that the spiritual circumcision of the heart is necessary so that this gift of divinity may flow in us.

The circumcision of the heart was first mentioned in Scripture in the Books of Moses:

> *And the Lord your God <u>will circumcise your heart</u> and the heart of your descendants, <u>to love the Lord</u> your God with all your heart and with all your soul, <u>that you may live</u>* (Deuteronomy 30:6).

Without the circumcision of the heart, it is difficult to truly love the Lord. If our hearts are not circumcised, life will not flow to us, for the verse says, 'Love the Lord ... that you may live'.

The lack of circumcision of the heart is due to the interaction between the spirit of the world, which creeps into us, and our fallen nature. It envelops the heart, causing it to become hardened and lose its spiritual sensitivity.

Therefore, the work of the cross is paramount in cutting off this foreskin (the uncircumcision of the heart) and crucifying the world and the flesh:

> But God forbid that I should boast except in the cross of our Lord Jesus Christ, <u>by whom the world has been crucified to me, and I to the world</u> (Galatians 6:14).

The more we are immersed in the cross, referred to as *baptism* in Luke 12:50, the more our hearts become tender and purified, allowing the gift of divinity to flow in us more.

For this reason, the Lord always drew the attention of His disciples to how the heart could become hardened. Stephen also confronted the leaders of the Jews, saying: *'You stiff-necked and uncircumcised in heart and ears'* (Acts 7:51).

Apostle Paul also wrote to the Romans saying:

> Circumcision is that of the heart, in the spirit, not in the letter; whose praise is not from men but from God (Romans 2:29).

The verses in Hebrews and Second Peter about partaking in the divine nature help us understand more about this gift.

> For we have become <u>partakers of Christ</u> if we hold the beginning of our confidence steadfast to the end (Hebrews 3:14).

At the beginning of our spiritual walk, we often find our love for God to be strong and vibrant. The Bible calls it the *first love*.[6] We also often have a simple, childlike faith that is strong and steadfast at the same time, and we obey the Lord with pleasure. However, as we face the cost of the narrow path and of bearing the cross, we stumble. Therefore, Jesus said, *'Blessed is he who is not offended because of Me'* (Matthew 11:6).

When we stumble, we start to slip back. Then, we may wake up for a while, but we slip back again, and so on. This spiritual fluctuation is harmful and hinders the flow of the gift of divinity. Because of this, Apostle Paul stresses that we have become partakers of Christ *'<u>if we hold</u> the beginning of our confidence <u>steadfast</u> to the end'*. Therefore, it is our responsibility *to hold steadfast*.

Then, the verse in 2 Peter 1:4 provides further insight into this matter:

---

[6] Revelation 2:4

By which have been given to us exceedingly great and pre-cious promises, that through these you may be <u>partakers of the divine nature</u>, having escaped the corruption that is in the world through lust.

This verse, which speaks about the gift of being partakers of the divine nature, is immediately followed by the following words:

But also <u>for this very reason</u>, <u>giving all diligence</u>, add to your faith virtue, to virtue knowledge (2 Peter 1:5).

The phrase *'for this very reason'* indicates that because we have become partakers of the divine nature and we need to escape from the corruption that is in the world, we ought to *give all diligence.*

The apostle repeats the idea of giving all diligence in verse 10 of the same chapter, saying:

Therefore, brethren, <u>be even more diligent</u> to make your call and election sure, for if you do these things you will never stumble (2 Peter 1:10).

Thus, verses 5 and 10 emphasise the importance and neces-sity of spiritual diligence.

In verses 5–10 of this chapter, Apostle Peter outlines seven important aspects that allow us to grow and be fruitful in the spiritual life: faith, virtue, knowledge, self-control, per-severance, godliness, brotherly kindness, and love. He emphasises the importance of diligence so that the corruption in the world may not creep into us and hinder the flow of such a precious gift.

The Amazing Riches That We Receive Through This Gift

Becoming the children of God is a great privilege, yet the Bible tells us about another amazing privilege related to this sonship relationship:

> *And if children, then heirs—<u>heirs of God</u> and joint heirs with Christ, if indeed we suffer with Him, that we may also be glorified together* (Romans 8:17).

> *Therefore you are no longer a slave but a son, and if a son, then <u>an heir of God</u> through Christ* (Galatians 4:7).

How amazing! We are heirs of God!

What does this mean?

We first need to understand that there is a difference between being the children of God, meaning being related to and belonging to God, and being His heirs.

To illustrate this difference, we can consider the following example. If, for instance, there was a famous, rich father and another famous but poor father. Both their sons would enjoy the privilege of being related to a great father as descendants. Yet only the rich father's son would inherit his father's riches.

Being children of the heavenly Father is a great privilege, but it only regards being His descendants, being related to Him and belonging to Him, but does not include being His heirs. Additionally, being granted the ability to be Christ-like and bear His characteristics as children of God is another great privilege. However, it is still only about being related to the Father and bearing His name and character-istics, but not about being His heirs who inherit from Him. Being His heirs is another privilege.

What do we inherit from God in Christ?

In Ephesians 1:18, we read:

> *The eyes of your understanding being enlightened; that you may know what is the hope of His calling, what are <u>the riches of the glory of His inheritance in the saints</u>.*

When we read the whole passage in Ephesians 1, we under-stand that Apostle Paul needed to pray for the Ephesians—who were the most spiritually mature church and to whom Paul wrote the most advanced theological epistle—that they might receive the spirit of wisdom and revelation (Ephesians 1:17) in order for the eyes of their hearts to be enlightened to perceive a great truth. After the eyes of their hearts were enlightened, he was able to tell them about *'the riches of the glory of* [God's] *inheritance in the saints'*.

Does God have an inheritance in us?

What kind of inheritance can we give Him when we are poor and dead because of our sins? Do we have anything to give?

Is it possible for us to give God an inheritance when He Himself is the source of all riches?

Doesn't this surprise us?!

What riches do we possess for God to find His inheritance in us?

Let me explain.

God grants us His grace as a free gift:

> *For by grace you have been saved through faith, and that not of yourselves; <u>it is the gift of God</u>* (Ephesians 2:8).

When we receive this free grace, it performs its work of great salvation inside us; thus, we begin to change and be transformed from fallen human beings into God's redeemed and beloved children. As we continue to *'work out* [our] *own salvation with fear and trembling'* (Philippians 2:12), grace becomes apparent in each person in various forms according to each one's gift, measure of grace, and calling. This results in the manifestation of the glorious and manifold grace in the redeemed. These varieties of grace will be displayed in the *heavenly exhibition* in the ages to come:

That in the ages to come He might <u>show</u> the exceeding riches of His grace in His kindness toward us in Christ Jesus (Ephesians 2:7).

In the original Greek language, the word *show* signifies an *exhibition*.

What a great mystery!

This will thus be the inheritance of God because we belong to Him; He has created us, bought us, and redeemed us. His Holy Spirit has also helped us to work out our salvation until grace has been glorified in us; thus, we have become glorified creatures. Therefore, God declares with great pleasure His inheritance in the saints. He says: "They are Mine; they are My great inheritance"—each according to his glorified redeemed picture, his supreme grace, and the mystery that has been deposited in him.

What a glorious scene, and what an amazing inheritance of God in the saints!

Not only this, but there is more. We mentioned earlier that we have become <u>*God's heirs*</u>. This means that every believer has a share in the inheritance of our heavenly Father. Every believer has a share in a holy glorified life that is full of light and glory; we have been entered into its glorious eternity.

How can this be, and how is this relevant to us?

In Psalm 92:12–15, we read:

The righteous shall flourish like a palm tree, he shall grow like a cedar in Lebanon. Those who are planted in the house of the Lord shall flourish in the courts of our God. They shall still bear fruit in old age; they shall be fresh and flourishing, to declare that the Lord is upright; He is my rock, and there is no unrighteousness in Him.

The righteous are like trees that flourish and bear fruits.

This is similar to what happens in the world of plants. When we plant a seed, this seed grows, becomes a tree, and bears fruits. We then take these fruits, plant them again, reap their fruits, and so on. The fruits we reap are of the same kind of seed we planted.

Similarly, in the spiritual world, we receive, by the Spirit, holy fruits from the lives of the saints. These saints have become God's inheritance; we share in this inheritance since we are God's heirs. Therefore, we receive holy fruits from the plant of their lives. Their lives bore fruits and were entered into God's holies so that we may receive them as new seeds in the new land of our lives. When we watch over this seed and water it, it grows anew inside us as a fruit of the same kind of life that those saints lived—a victorious life that bears witness to Christ in various forms.

Therefore, every saint, righteous person, and martyr adds new riches, by the grace inside him, to the inheritance of the one Church—God's inheritance in His Church, in His saints. Then, we take from this inheritance. Hence, our riches increase and the glory increases since it is the unlimited glory of God.

II. The Fullness of Fruitfulness

T he fruits that result from a life in which divinity flows
are quite remarkable:

1. The Outer Conduct

*That you may walk worthy of the Lord, fully pleasing Him,
being fruitful in every good work and increasing in the
knowledge of God; strengthened with all might, according to
His glorious power, for all patience and longsuffering with
joy* (Colossians 1:10–11).

According to the original Greek text, the phrase strengthened with all might means enabled whenever necessary and
needed.

The phrase according to His glorious power refers to the
power of God who is the source that enables us.

– *For all patience and longsuffering*

Longsuffering is different from patience because it refers to
patience in times of distress, burdens, and oppositions.

– *With joy*

There is joy despite all the hardships and difficulties. How
amazing! Yes, this is real and true because these are the
fruits of the gift of divinity!

2. The Inner Life

Therefore, as the elect of God, holy and beloved, put on tender mercies, kindness, humility, meekness, longsuffering; bearing with one another, and forgiving one another, if anyone has a complaint against another; even as Christ forgave you, so you also must do. But above all these things put on love, which is the bond of perfection. And let the peace of God rule in your hearts, to which also you were called in one body; and be thankful (Colossians 3:12–15).

This passage portrays an inner holy life that bears the fruits of victory in daily confrontations through love, forgiveness, peace, and thanksgiving.

3. The Attitude or Motive Behind Our Conduct

And whatever you do in word or deed, do all in the name of the Lord Jesus, giving thanks to God the Father through Him (Colossians 3:17).

And whatever you do, do it heartily, as to the Lord and not to men (Colossians 3:23).

These verses portray a picture of a pure and righteous heart with honest and sincere attitudes and motives directed upwards towards God to please Him.

They are attitudes and motives free from any hypocrisy.

They are attitudes that spring out of a pure heart.

4. Holy Zeal in Ministry

Him we preach [Christ in you, the hope of glory], *warning every man and teaching every man in all wisdom, that we may present every man perfect in Christ Jesus. To this end I also labour, striving according to His working which works in me mightily* (Colossians 1:28, 29).

This passage reflects the holy zeal of the apostle. It is directed towards every person (all people), with the desire to present every man perfect in Christ. The apostle is ready to sacrifice and pour out himself, striving to fulfil this holy purpose.

5. The Life of Worship—Diligence in Worship

Let the word of Christ dwell in you richly in all wisdom, teaching and admonishing one another in psalms and hymns and spiritual songs, singing with grace in your hearts to the Lord (Colossians 3:16).

Continue [meaning uninterruptedly] *earnestly in prayer, being vigilant in it with thanksgiving; meanwhile praying also for us, that God would open to us a door for the word, to speak the mystery of Christ, for which I am also in chains* (Colossians 4:2, 3).

Epaphras, who is one of you, a bondservant of Christ, greets you, always labouring fervently for you in prayers, that you may stand perfect and complete in all the will of God (Colossians 4:12).

This reflects a picture of a true and victorious worship life. It is an inner life of worship, desiring the continuous infilling of the Holy Spirit.

According to scholars, Colossians 3:16, mentioned earlier, is parallel to Ephesians 5:19.

Speaking to one another in psalms and hymns and spiritual songs, singing and making melody in your heart to the Lord (Ephesians 5:19).

This again reflects a vigilant life of continuous prayer, praying for others to be filled with *'all the will of God'* (Colossians 4:12) and to minister the Word of God (Colossians 4:3).

III. The Fullness of God's Will

(All the Will of God)

In Colossians 1:9, we read:

> *For this reason we also, since the day we heard it, do not cease to pray for you, and to ask that you may be filled with <u>the knowledge of His will</u> in all wisdom and spiritual understanding.*

> — *That you may be filled with the knowledge of His will*

According to the original language, these words mean to receive knowledge that increases continually through fellowship with God, not through studies and intellectual knowledge; consequently, the will of God will be revealed more and more until it reaches its fullness.

Also, in Colossians 4:12, we read:

> *Epaphras, who is one of you, a bondservant of Christ, greets you, always <u>labouring fervently for you in prayers,</u> that you may stand perfect and complete <u>in all the will of God</u>* (Colossians 4:12).

These words signify the presence of an opponent who hinders Epaphras in his spiritual labour as he strives to reveal all the will of God (the full will, not just part of it) to the Church of God. However, Epaphras labours and strives against this opposition. Of course the opposition comes from the enemy who tries to hinder even part of God's will in the life of believers, if he fails to hinder all the will of God.

What is the connection between our inner life and discovering God's will and the fullness of His will?

God's will is given to man in the form of a mystical divine book:

> *And I saw the dead, small and great, standing before God, and books were opened. And another book was opened, which is the Book of Life. And the dead were judged according to their works, <u>by the things which were written in the books</u>* (Revelation 20:12).

Notice that there is *the Book of Life* and also other books which are *the books of God's will for man.* These books reveal how much of the divine purposes each person accomplished during his life on earth.

One's life is a story that God has written for man since eternity:

> *We finish our years like <u>a sigh</u>* [or like a story, according to the Hebrew language] (Psalm 90:9b).

Like any book, this book or story consists of chapters. Thus, we need to know the chapters of the book of our lives according to God's mind. These chapters are the chapters of God's will for us. They are, of course, related to the new spiritual man that has been granted to us in Jesus Christ:

Therefore, if anyone is in Christ, he is a new creation; old things have passed away; behold, all things have become new (2 Corinthians 5:17).

For we are His workmanship, created in Christ Jesus for good works, which God prepared beforehand that we should walk in them (Ephesians 2:10).

If indeed you have heard Him and have been taught by Him, as the truth is in Jesus: that you put off, concerning your former conduct, the old man which grows corrupt according to the deceitful lusts, and be renewed in the spirit of your mind, and that you put on the new man which was created according to God, in true righteousness and holiness (Ephesians 4:21–24).

Since you have put off the old man with his deeds, and have put on the new man who is renewed in knowledge according to the image of Him who created him (Colossians 3:9b, 10).

Thus, the chapters of the book of one's life, the story of one's life according to God's will, are revealed to the inner man.

These references clarify that the inner man grows gradually. The more we take off the old man, the more the new man grows and shines. This, in turn, reflects on how much we obey God, keep His commandments, and walk in the Spirit.

The more the new man grows and broadens, the more it becomes able to receive from the Holy Spirit a new chapter in the book of one's life story—the mystical book in which God's will for the person is written and revealed. One should perceive it, obey it, and carry out the Kingdom work planned for him by God.

For we are His workmanship, created in Christ Jesus for good works, which God prepared beforehand that we should walk in them (Ephesians 2:10).

The Holy Spirit is the Person of the Trinity responsible for opening and revealing this book to us bit by bit. Thus, the more we obey the Holy Spirit and learn His language, the more this sealed book is opened for us:

Whom will he teach knowledge? And whom will he make to understand the message? Those just weaned from milk? Those just drawn from the breasts? For precept must be upon precept, precept upon precept, line upon line, line upon line, here a little, there a little (Isaiah 28:9, 10).

The whole vision has become to you like the words of a book that is sealed, which men deliver to one who is literate, saying, "Read this, please." And he says, "I cannot, for it is sealed." Then the book is delivered to one who is illiterate, saying, "Read this, please." And he says, "I am not literate" (Isaiah 29:11, 12).

The sealed book is also opened based on our renewed trust in the blood of the Lamb (Hebrews 10:19; Revelation 5:1–5; Revelation 12:11) because the Lamb of God was granted to open all the closed books. The Holy Spirit then teaches us how to read them.

Therefore, brethren, having boldness to enter the Holiest by the blood of Jesus (Hebrews 10:19).

And I saw in the right hand of Him who sat on the throne a scroll written inside and on the back, sealed with seven seals. Then I saw a strong angel proclaiming with a loud voice, "Who is worthy to open the scroll and to loose its seals?" And no one in heaven or on the earth or under the earth was able to open the scroll, or to look at it. So I wept much, because no one was found worthy to open and read the scroll, or to look at it. But one of the elders said to me, "Do not weep. Behold, the Lion of the tribe of Judah, the Root of David, has prevailed to open the scroll and to loose its seven seals" (Revelation 5:1–5).

And they overcame him by the blood of the Lamb and by the word of their testimony, and they did not love their lives to the death (Revelation 12:11).

Printed in Great Britain
by Amazon